HAMLYN - COLOURFAX

PAPER FUN

ANN LOESCHER

CONTENTS

HAMLYN

MATERIALS

Paper comes in so many different colours, textures and thicknesses that, with the help of a few other simple materials, there is no limit to the exciting things you can make. And what's more, it's cheap and easy to find, just look around you and use your imagination – it's all part of the fun!

There are many ways to get paper free. You can ask in shops and offices but much of what you will need can be found at home.

Cereal packets are good as lightweight card and cardboard boxes can be used where heavier card is required. See-through plastic bags in different colours are ideal for stained-glass style ornaments.

Collect unwanted wrapping paper, silver or gold foil (often found in packets of tea) and old magazines and newspapers. You can sometimes buy ends of runs of wallpaper quite cheaply to add to your store of materials. Use a large cardboard box to keep your collection flat and uncreased.

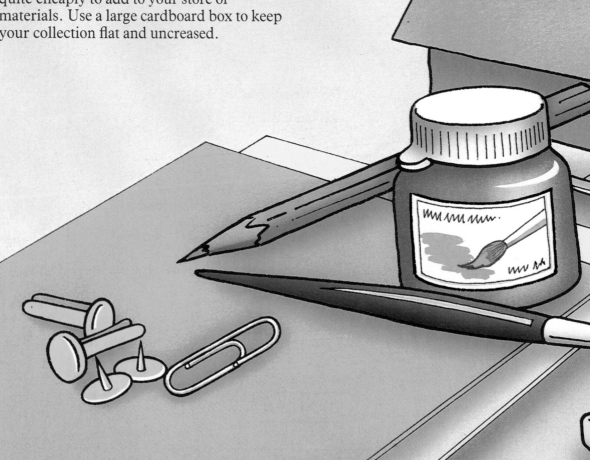

EQUIPMENT

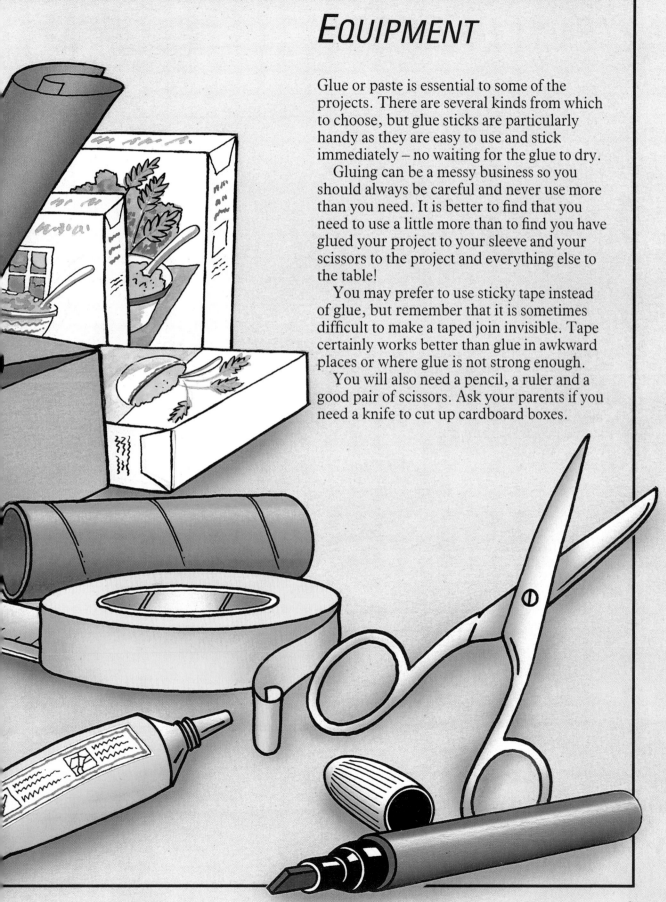

Glue or paste is essential to some of the projects. There are several kinds from which to choose, but glue sticks are particularly handy as they are easy to use and stick immediately – no waiting for the glue to dry.

Gluing can be a messy business so you should always be careful and never use more than you need. It is better to find that you need to use a little more than to find you have glued your project to your sleeve and your scissors to the project and everything else to the table!

You may prefer to use sticky tape instead of glue, but remember that it is sometimes difficult to make a taped join invisible. Tape certainly works better than glue in awkward places or where glue is not strong enough.

You will also need a pencil, a ruler and a good pair of scissors. Ask your parents if you need a knife to cut up cardboard boxes.

PAPER ON THE MOVE

FOLDED GLIDERS

You will need: 2 rectangular pieces of paper about 20 cm by 30 cm

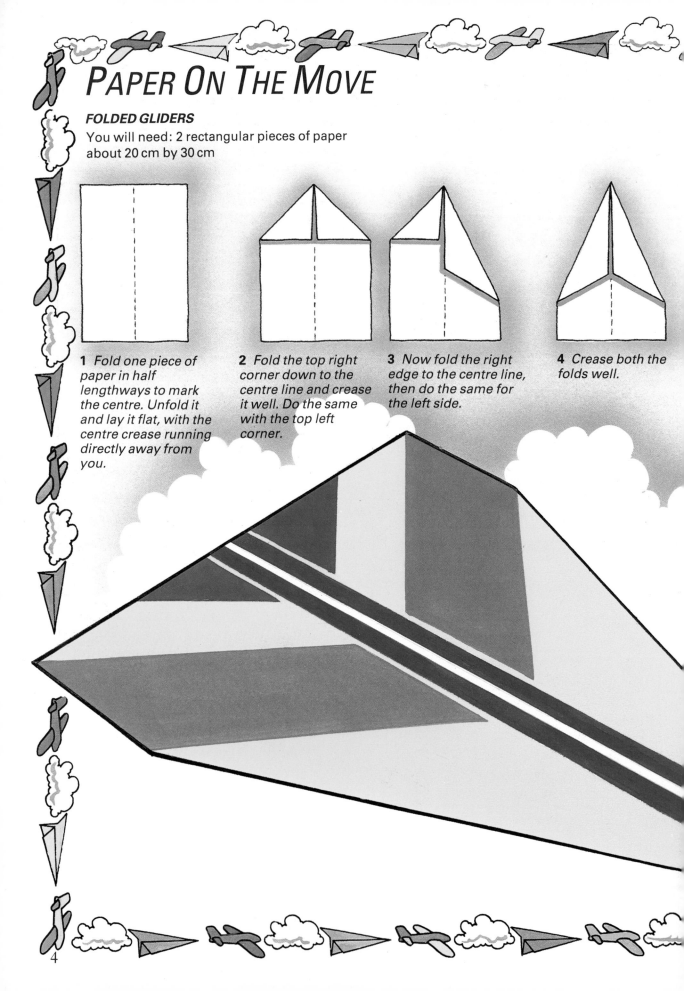

1 Fold one piece of paper in half lengthways to mark the centre. Unfold it and lay it flat, with the centre crease running directly away from you.

2 Fold the top right corner down to the centre line and crease it well. Do the same with the top left corner.

3 Now fold the right edge to the centre line, then do the same for the left side.

4 Crease both the folds well.

You can give your glider bigger wings to help it fly even better. Take a similar piece of paper and repeat steps 1 to 4. Slide your glider inside, under the flaps of the second sheet until the tip is snugly in place.

You can fasten the two sections together with a little glue, then gently throw the glider high into the air for long distance flying.

5 *Fold the paper in half along the centre line so that the flaps are inside.*

6 *Fold each side back, again lengthways, about 15 mm from the centre fold. The glider is now ready to fly.*

FINGER PROPELLER

You will need: A sheet of paper 7.5 cm by 15 cm. Make sure the paper size and folds are exact

1 *Make folds along all 4 sides of the paper about 6 mm from the edge.*

2 *Where the folds cross at the corners, flatten them a little more and pinch the corners upwards and outwards to form sharp points. It should look like a shallow dish with very pointed corners.*

To make your finger propeller spin, hold the paper between the tips of your index fingers. Your right finger should be on the centre of the flat side and your left finger should be on the centre of the side with the points.

With plenty of room for a straight run, turn your back to the direction you intend to run in. Still holding the paper between your fingertips, point your right index straight ahead. Turn around quickly but smoothly and start running. Remove your left finger and the propeller will spin on the end of your right finger as you run.

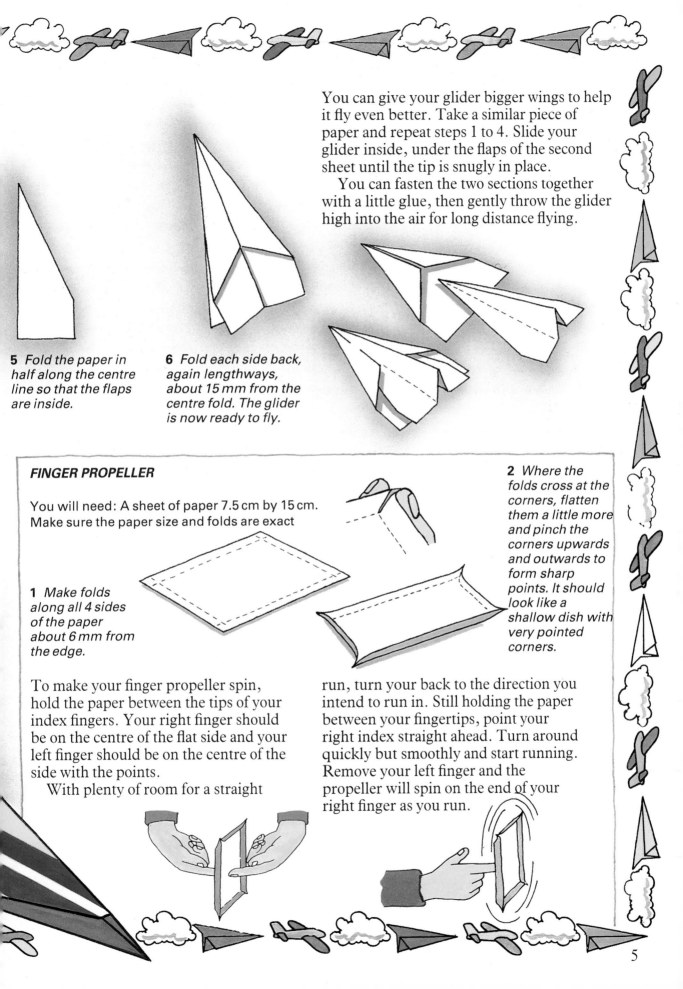

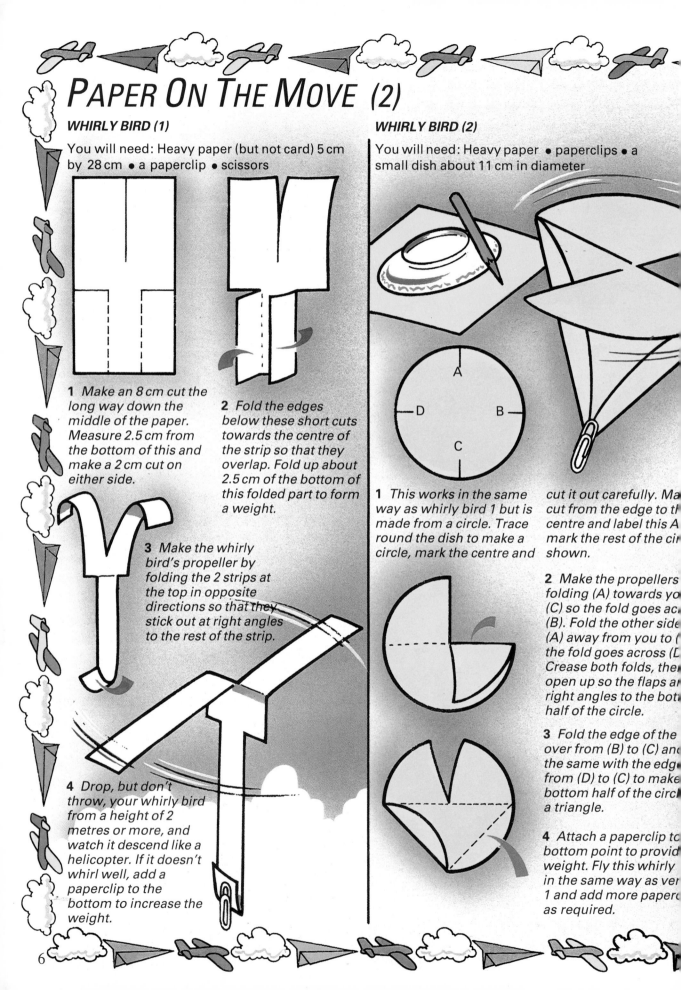

PAPER ON THE MOVE (2)

WHIRLY BIRD (1)

You will need: Heavy paper (but not card) 5 cm by 28 cm ● a paperclip ● scissors

1 Make an 8 cm cut the long way down the middle of the paper. Measure 2.5 cm from the bottom of this and make a 2 cm cut on either side.

2 Fold the edges below these short cuts towards the centre of the strip so that they overlap. Fold up about 2.5 cm of the bottom of this folded part to form a weight.

3 Make the whirly bird's propeller by folding the 2 strips at the top in opposite directions so that they stick out at right angles to the rest of the strip.

4 Drop, but don't throw, your whirly bird from a height of 2 metres or more, and watch it descend like a helicopter. If it doesn't whirl well, add a paperclip to the bottom to increase the weight.

WHIRLY BIRD (2)

You will need: Heavy paper ● paperclips ● a small dish about 11 cm in diameter

1 This works in the same way as whirly bird 1 but is made from a circle. Trace round the dish to make a circle, mark the centre and cut it out carefully. Ma[...] cut from the edge to th[...] centre and label this A [...] mark the rest of the cir[...] shown.

2 Make the propellers [...] folding (A) towards yo[...] (C) so the fold goes ac[...] (B). Fold the other side [...] (A) away from you to ([...] the fold goes across (D[...] Crease both folds, the[...] open up so the flaps a[...] right angles to the bot[...] half of the circle.

3 Fold the edge of the [...] over from (B) to (C) an[...] the same with the edg[...] from (D) to (C) to make [...] bottom half of the circ[...] a triangle.

4 Attach a paperclip to [...] bottom point to provid[...] weight. Fly this whirly [...] in the same way as ver[...] 1 and add more paperc[...] as required.

BALLOON JET MONORAIL

You will need: An empty kitchen towel roll ● a long piece of smooth string ● a paperclip ● a large balloon (with attached siren whistle if possible) ● lightweight paper ● a tube of light card 1.75 cm in diameter and 1.75 cm long ● tape

1 Lightly glue the towel roll and wrap in the lightweight paper to cover it, keeping the ends clear. Paint or decorate it as you like, perhaps as a train or rocket.

2 Securely tape the small card tube beneath the back end of the towel roll. If you are using a balloon with a tubular whistle simply tape the whistle to the roll in the same way.

3 Thread the long string through the towel roll and tie it between 2 secure objects such as a table leg and door handle or 2 trees. The string must be tight and level to ensure that the monorail works well.
   Push the open end of the balloon through the small tube with the nozzle pointing to the rear.

4 Blow up the balloon and, carefully holding the nozzle closed, use a paperclip to fasten its rim to the rear opening of the towel roll. Then release the balloon. As it deflates, the jet of air will push the roll along the string. A gentle push will speed it on its way.

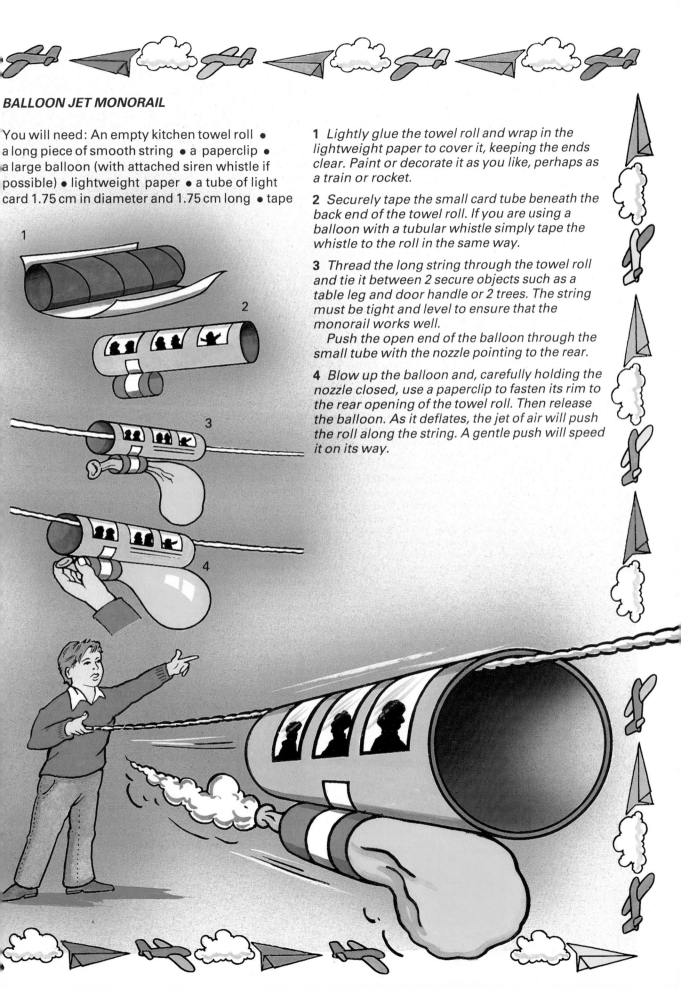

PAPIER-MÂCHÉ

Papier-mâché is quite messy to work with so you will need plenty of room. Choose somewhere where no-one will mind a mess and place a waterproof covering on the floor or table. The paste takes several hours to dry between layers, so you will need to be able to leave your work out where it won't be in anyone's way.

Tearing paper
Paper has a grain like wood. Tearing and folding along the grain is neater and easier than across the grain. Tear some old newspapers into fairly even strips about 2 cm wide and no longer than 12–15 cm long. Longer strips are harder to work with. Final layers will require even narrower strips.

Mixing paste
Wallpaper paste is best and you can buy this in small quantities. Mix according to the instructions and only make a small batch at a time as it does not keep for long. You can make your own paste from flour and water, but it can sometimes go mouldy.

Building up layers
Papier-mâché is a means of building up overlapping layers of paper soaked in paste. When the paste dries, the paper hardens. Build up the layers carefully, keeping to the planned shape of what you are making. Make sure that each layer is completely dry before starting the next. A layer should not be more than three or four sheets of paper thick.

After removing the paper from the paste, draw it gently between two fingers of one hand to clean off surplus paste. Smooth the pasted strip onto your model without leaving air bubbles or creases.

HOT-AIR BALLOON

You will need: Papier-mâché • balloon • paints or coloured markers • thin string • a small plastic pot or yoghurt carton • coloured paper

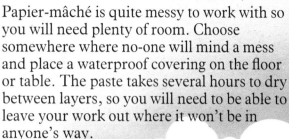

1 *Blow up the balloon to the size you want. Starting at the opposite end to the nozzle, apply the strips of papier-mâché until all the balloon has been evenly covered, leaving a circle about 5–7.5 cm in diameter at the nozzle end.*

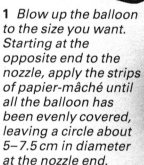

2 *When it is dry, add another layer and repeat until the fourth or fifth layer. Take special care to make the last layer as smooth as possible. Once this is dry, pop the balloon and remove it. Carefully lay more strips around the opening to build up a neat finish.*

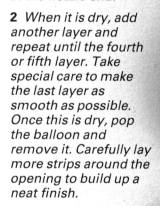

3 *Use short strips of papier-mâché to fix a rubber band to the end opposite the opening.*

SPACE HELMET

You will need: Papier-mâché • large balloon • large piece of thin card • sticky tape • 2 yoghurt pots • paints or markers

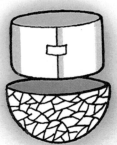

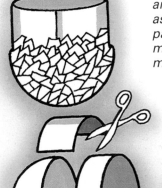

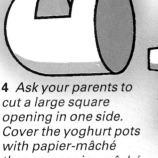

3 Insert the card tube and tape into position as shown. Cover with papier-mâché to match the part already made.

1 Blow up the balloon until it is larger than your head and apply a layer of papier-mâché until half way up the balloon. When dry, add another layer and repeat for 4 layers.

2 When the final layer is dry, cut a strip of thin card about 25 cm wide and long enough to fit loosely around your head. Tape it into a tube. Pop the balloon and remove it from the papier-mâché.

4 Ask your parents to cut a large square opening in one side. Cover the yoghurt pots with papier-mâché then use papier-mâché strips to fix a yoghurt pot to each side of the opening and paint the helmet.

4 While this is drying, glue coloured paper to the plastic pot. Taking great care, use a skewer or the point of a pair of scissors to make 4 holes at equal distances in the rim.

5 Cut 4 pieces of string 10 cm long and tie a simple knot in the end of each. Thread one through each of the holes in the pot from the inside.

6 When the papier-mâché globe is completely dry, make 4 holes in the rim of the opening at equal distances.
   Thread the pieces of string through from the outside and tie a knot in the end of each, making sure that the pot hangs level. You can now decorate the outside of your hot-air balloon.

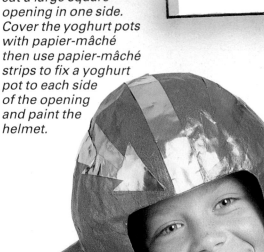

POP-UP CARDS

If you are going to post your card, make it to fit a standard size envelope. Huge or strangely shaped home-made envelopes may mean extra postage!

A greetings card opens from the right like a book or from the bottom. It can be of single thickness with one fold, or double thickness with two folds. There are different ways of doing pop-up cards. Something can pop up from the top, out of the centre fold or a part can be moved with a tab.

HALLOWEEN CARD WITH BAT

You will need: Heavy paper 10 cm × 20 cm ● lightweight paper ● coloured markers ● glue

1 Trace the bat pattern onto the heavy paper and fold the paper in half the short way.

3 Use bright colours for the eyes and background. Draw a scary background, perhaps with a bright moon and a spooky castle.

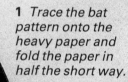

2 Cut out the bat and crease the centre fold firmly. Following the dotted lines shown, fold the bat's wings forward and then back, then forward again. Vary the angle of the folds as shown, keeping the bat as symmetrical as possible.

4 Fold the card and fold the bat, then slip the bat into the closed card to find the right position. Hold the wing tips in place with your thumbs as you open the card. Glue the wing tips in place. Now you can write your message.

BIRTHDAY CARD

You will need: Heavy paper ● lightweight paper ● glue

1 Start with paper that is twice as big as the card will be. Fold it in half one way, then in half again the other way.

3 Stick the tab to the middle of the card. Stick decorations and candles on the cake. Cut a pull tab 12 mm wide and long enough to reach from the cake to beyond the side of the card.

2 Cut out a cake shape from the lightweight paper. It should be a little less than half as wide as the part of the card you will glue it to. Allow enough paper for a tab about 6 mm wide and almost as high as the cake along the left of the cake.

CUT

4 Flip the cake over to face the right way and mark where its right edge touches the card. Flip it onto the wrong side. Unfold the card and cut a 12 mm vertical slit in the top layer 12 mm to the left of this mark.

5 Slip the pull tab through the slit and out between the layers of paper. Fold over the end of the tab inside the card and carefully glue to the back of the cake.

Flip the cake to the left and trim the outside end of the tab to 12 mm. Write 'PULL' on the end and finish your card.

ROLLING EYES CARD

You will need: Heavy paper ● paper fastener ● marker pens

1 Make the double fold as shown.

2 Mark the card where you want the face to be and open the card again. Draw the face or cut one from paper and stick it in place. Leave out the eyes.

3 Cut 2 holes for the eyes and poke a tiny hole through the nose. Cut a circle of paper about the same size as the head and make a tiny hole in the centre.

Pass the paper fastener through the holes in the card and the paper circle. Bend the prongs so that the circle turns freely. Draw the eyes through the eye holes onto the paper circle.

4 Cut a strip of paper about 12 mm wide and long enough to reach from the circle to outside the card. Glue one end to the circle and draw an arrow on the other to show how to work it.

DRESSING UP AND DISGUISES

BOWLER HAT

You will need: Two large pieces of thick paper • ruler • scissors • sticky tape or glue • medium-sized plate • decoration materials

Make the crown of the hat first. Cut a piece of paper about 20 cm wide and long enough to go round your head with an overlap of 2 cm. Draw a line along one long edge of the paper about 5 cm from the edge. Cut strips about 2.5 cm wide from the other long edge to this line. Fasten the ends of the uncut edge to make a band that fits around your head. Take two opposite strips and stick the ends together. Then stick another pair of opposite strips together on top. Continue until all are stacked up and glued.

Now make the brim. Draw around the plate on the other sheet of paper and cut the circle out. Stand the crown of the hat in the middle of this circle and draw around it. Then cut out that circle to make the hole in the middle of the brim.

Cut about 20 to 30 flaps about 1.5 cm deep at regular intervals around the bottom of the crown of the hat, and bend them all outwards as shown.

Slip the brim over the crown and on to the flaps. If it fits too tightly trim it until it fits, then stick it to the flaps on the crown.

Paint it black if you want a bowler hat or use bright colours and decorate with a big paper flower or feathers.

CROWN

You will need: A large piece of thick paper • scissors • sticky tape or glue • paints • decoration materials

Cut a strip of paper long enough to go around your head with an overlap of 2 cm and as wide as you want your crown to be high. Draw the shape you want on the paper then cut it out. If you want the crown to be symmetrical, fold the paper in half, widthways, draw on one side, then cut through both pieces together. You can decorate your crown by sticking on paper jewels. Or cut holes and stick coloured cellophane over them on the inside. When you have finished decorating the crown, fasten the ends together around your head with tape or glue.

You can make a Red Indian's head-dress the same way – just cut or stick on feather shapes instead.

CONICAL HAT

You will need: A large sheet of stiff paper • sticky tape or glue • decoration materials • 2 lengths of ribbon or tape

Roll the paper into a tall cone. Hold it in shape and try it on your head. If it does not fit, try again. When it does fit, tape or glue it in position. Make two holes in opposite sides of the bottom of the hat through which you can thread lengths of tape to tie under your chin. Make a knot in each end on the inside of the hat. You can make the holes stronger by sticking small pieces of paper on the back of those areas first.

Now decorate the hat any way you like. If you want a brim, follow the directions for putting a brim on the bowler hat.

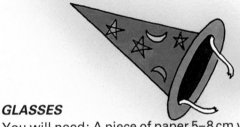

GLASSES

You will need: A piece of paper 5–8 cm wide and long enough to reach from behind one ear, across your forehead to the other • scissors • pencil • sticky tape or glue

Fold the paper in half and cut off the corner of the fold. Open out, try on and adjust if necessary. Fold again, draw half a pair of glasses on one side and cut out. Unfold, flatten across the nose and fold the arms back.

Strengthen the nose and where the arms bend with pieces of paper and use coloured cellophane for lenses.

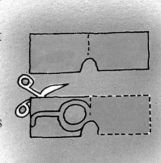

MASK

You will need: Thick paper or light card • sticky tape or glue • stapler • pencil • decorating materials • piece of elastic

Cut the paper into a rectangle a little larger than your face. Lightly fold it in half the long way to mark the centre and round off the bottom for the chin. Make two 4 cm long cuts from the bottom about 3 cm either side of the centre fold.

Pull in the edges of the side flaps and glue to the middle one to form the chin. Place the mask over your face and mark where your eyes, nose and mouth are. Draw on the features you want and make eyeholes to see through. You can also cut a flap to make room for your nose.

Decorate your mask as you like. You can add paper eyebrows, a nose, teeth, lips and horns etc. Score and fold each shape to make them stand out from the mask.

Tie a knot in each end of the elastic and staple it to the sides of the mask. Extra pieces of paper glued to the stapling points will give them extra strength.

CLOWN BOW-TIE

You will need: A sheet of colourful wrapping paper • scissors • sticky tape or glue • a safety pin

Cut 2 pieces of paper – one about 13 cm by 38 cm, the other about 8 cm by 15 cm. Fold the large piece in half widthways to mark the centre, then unfold it and place it wrong side up. Fold each end to the centre and glue.

With the small piece of paper wrong side up, fold each long edge over about 2 cm to give it strength. Pick up the first piece and lightly squeeze the middle to form a bow-tie shape, then wrap the smaller piece round and glue in place.

MOUSTACHES AND BEARDS

You will need: Stiff paper • pencil • scissors • sticky tape or glue

Moustache

Cut a piece of paper about the size of your lower face. Fold it in half, draw half a moustache shape then cut it out.

Make a small nose clip by cutting out a paper circle about 1.5 cm in diameter. Make a small cut in the edge and cut a smaller circle from the middle. Round the corners of the cut to form a smooth horseshoe shape and adjust to fit. Glue it to the back of the moustache with the nose clip upwards.

Beard

Cut a piece of paper wide enough to reach from ear to ear and as long as you wish the beard to be. Fold the paper in half and draw half a beard with earpieces as shown. Cut out the shape and unfold.

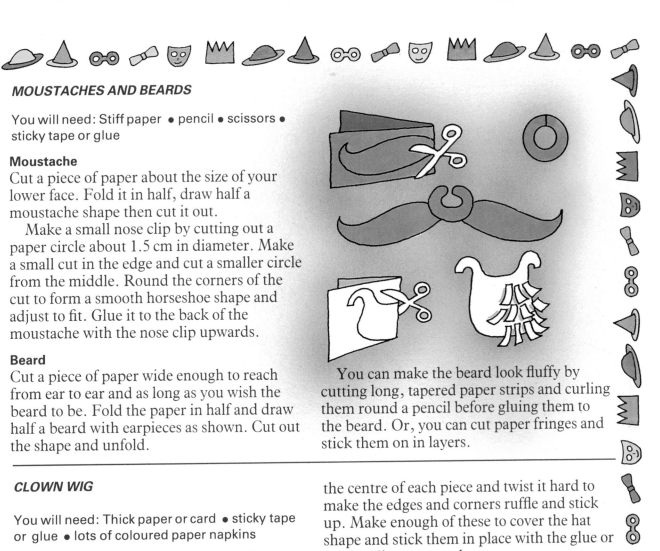

You can make the beard look fluffy by cutting long, tapered paper strips and curling them round a pencil before gluing them to the beard. Or, you can cut paper fringes and stick them on in layers.

CLOWN WIG

You will need: Thick paper or card • sticky tape or glue • lots of coloured paper napkins

Cut and fasten a strip of heavy paper long enough to form a band around your head. Cut 4 more strips to reach from one side of the band over your head to the other. Glue one from side to side, one from back to front, and the other 2 in between to form a 'hat'.

To make the hair, open the paper napkins and cut them into quarters. If they are double thickness napkins, separate the layers. Pinch the centre of each piece and twist it hard to make the edges and corners ruffle and stick up. Make enough of these to cover the hat shape and stick them in place with the glue or tape until no spaces show.

TRICKS AND PUZZLES

MOBIUS TRICK STRIP

You will need: Lightweight paper ● pencil ● scissors ● glue

Cut a strip of paper about 3 cm wide and 30 cm long. Bring the 2 ends together, twisting *one* of them over before gluing them to each other. You will now have a twisted loop of paper.

You can prove that your trick strip only has ONE side, not 2 like ordinary paper! Just draw a line along the strip without lifting the pencil from the paper. You will come back to the beginning of the lines, but although you never turned the paper over, the line will be on both sides!

Now cut along the line with scissors. When you reach the start of your cut the loop should fall into two pieces. But it doesn't! It makes one bigger loop instead.

Make another trick strip, but this time make your cut 5 mm from one edge. You will eventually pass the beginning of your cut on the other side of the strip. Stop when you meet it again. You will be surprised to see that you now have one loop of paper passing through another!

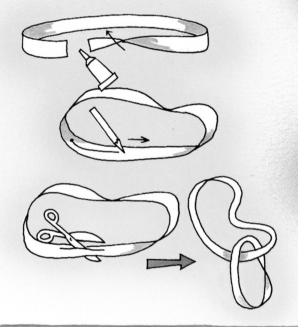

INSIDE-OUT CUBE

You will need: Paper ● tape ● glue ● pencil and coloured markers

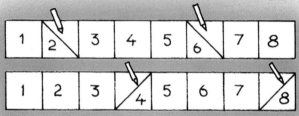

1 Cut a strip of paper 5 cm wide and 40 cm long. Mark the strip in 5 cm squares and number them 1 to 8 from left to right on both *sides*. Each square must have the same number on each side. Draw a line along both edges of each end of the strip.

2 With the numbered squares running left to right, draw a diagonal line from the top left corner to the bottom right corner of squares 2 and 6. Flip the strip over and draw in diagonals from top right to bottom left on squares 4 and 8.

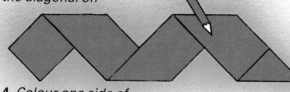

3 Flip the strip back to the first side again. Fold the strip towards you along the diagonal you drew on squares 2 and 6. Fold the strip away from you along the diagonal on squares 4 and 8. Carefully open each of the triangles you have made to glue them down. You will now have a strip of 4 squares and 4 triangles.

4 Colour one side of the strip and lay it in front of you coloured side down, with the square numbered 1 on the left.

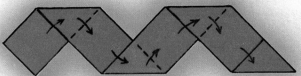

5 To form the cube, fold each of the squares and triangles from left to right, at right angles to the next shape. Continue until you fold triangle 8 over the top to complete the cube. The 2 marked ends should meet. Tape them together edge to edge.

6 To turn your cube inside out, place the cube on the table with a side with a diagonal opening running towards and away from you. Gently push the right half away from you and down, and the left half towards you and down. The cube will collapse and form a flat square with a corner towards you.

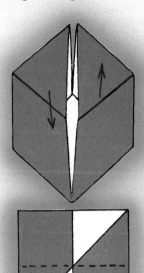

7 Turn the square clockwise so that its nearest side runs from left to right. Fold the top half over to make a rectangle.

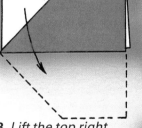

8 Lift the top right corner and open it downwards and towards you to make a white lozenge shape. Hold the top left corner down and fold the right half of the lozenge under the left half to form a rectangle with a short edge towards you.

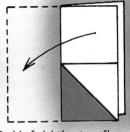 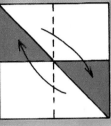

9 Unfold the top flap of the rectangle, like opening a book, to make a large square again. Turn the square to the right until the diagonal runs towards and away from you once again.

10 Slide the diagonal edges in opposite directions and lift into a cube again. Ease the coloured inside down. The cube will be inside out!

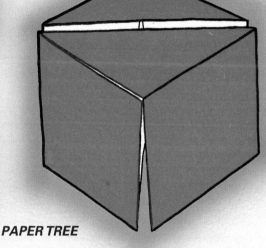

PAPER TREE

Turn a newspaper back into the tree it was made from.

You will need: Newspaper • scissors • tape

1 Roll 3 or 4 sheets of newspaper into a tube. Fix with tape in the middle and one end.

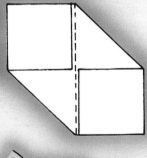

2 Make 4 15 cm cuts in the untaped end as shown. Stand tube on end, fold back 4 strips and gently pull inside sections upwards.

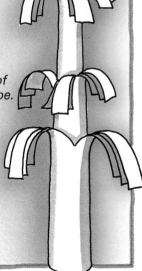

ORIGAMI

JUMPING FROG

You will need: Lightweight card 5 cm by 8 cm

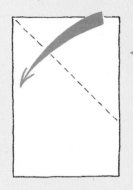

1 Lay the paper on a flat surface with a short edge nearest you. Fold the top right corner to the left hand edge and crease the fold. Then unfold it again.

2 Fold the top left corner down and across to the right hand edge. Crease and unfold again.

3 Fold the top part away from you so that the crease runs horizontally through the point where the other two creases cross. Repeat steps 1–3 a few times to flex the crease.

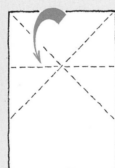

4 The paper should now cup slightly with the horizontal crease raised. Hold the paper down with your thumbs and slip your index fingers under each end of the horizontal crease.

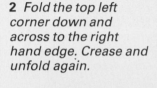

5 Ease the edges inwards and towards you to make a triangular sandwich. Press the triangle flat, then fold the left and right points of the top triangle upwards and

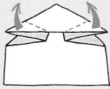

inwards to form the frog's front legs.

6 Fold each side of the long bottom piece of the paper into the centre so that the edges meet.

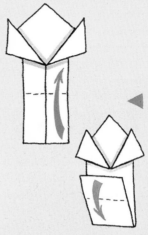

7 Fold the bottom of this section up halfway, then back down a quarter of the way in a reverse fold. This forms the back legs. You can now decorate your frog.

8 To make the frog jump, stand it on its legs on a flat surface. Place your finger on the top centre of its rump and press down lightly. Slip your finger off smartly to release the frog.

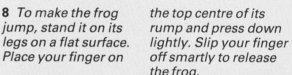

POPPER

You will need: Rectangular piece of lightweight paper

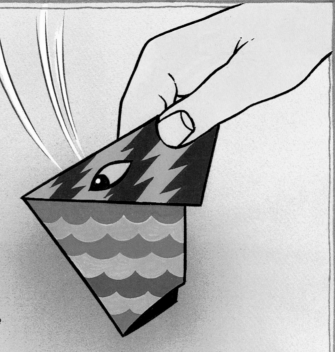

1 Fold the paper lengthways, crease and then unfold.

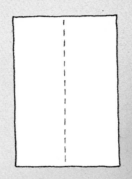

2 Fold each of the corners in to the centre crease to make a lozenge shape.

3 Fold the lozenge in half lengthways along the centre crease.

4 Fold it in half again the opposite way by bringing the point nearest you up to the furthest point. Unfold again.

5 Turn the whole shape over away from you so that the points change places and the horizontal crease rises upwards.

6 Fold each point inwards so that their long edges lie along the horizontal crease. You should now have a square divided into 2 triangles.

7 Fold the upper triangle away from you along the horizontal crease.

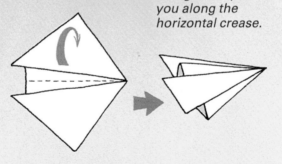

8 Hold the popper by the 2 free points and snap your hand sharply downwards.

If it doesn't 'pop', loosen the inner folds slightly and try again.

ORIGAMI (2)

FLYING CRANE

You will need: A piece of fairly heavy paper
15–20 cm square • marker pens

1 *Fold the paper in half along a diagonal, open it and repeat along the other diagonal.*

2 *Turn the paper over and fold it in half from side to side. Open it and repeat for the other 2 sides.*

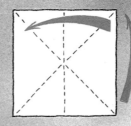

3 *Place the paper in front of you with a corner pointing towards you and the centre raised. Lightly slide the left and right points towards the centre, and flatten the nearest and furthest squares on top of one another.*

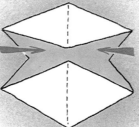

4 *You should now have a small square. Lay it on the table so that the open-pointed end and the diagonal crease point towards you. Each of the 2 nearest sides consists of 4 layers of paper. Fold up the top 2 on each side to lie along the diagonal crease.*

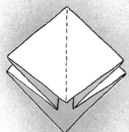

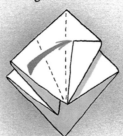

5 *Fold the far corner of the square down over the far edges of the 2 triangular flaps you made in step 4.*

6 *Unfold the step 4 flaps.*

7 *Hold down all the points facing you and pull just the top point up and away from you.*

8 *Push in the 2 sides towards the centre to form a long, flat diamond shape and crease. The point nearest you should lie over a small square.*

9 *Turn the paper over with the same point away from you and the square now on top of the diamond.*

10 Fold the 2 nearest edges of the square in and up to the centre crease as in step 4. Fold the furthest point of the square over these new flaps and open them out again as in steps 5 and 6.

11 Take the top layer of the points facing you, fold it up and away as step 7. Press in the sides and flatten as step 8.

12 You should now have just 2 points nearest to you. Fold

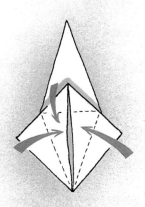

these up and out so that the inner edge lies along the centre horizontal crease to form a 'boat' shape.

15 Use your other hand to flatten this shape so it points to the right. Fold the top half of this small diamond over the bottom half and flatten. Do the same for the left side.

16 Pick up the model and press down the tip of the right point and reverse fold it to form the head.

13 Unfold them again, turn the diamond over and repeat step 12. Unfold them. Put a pencil mark on the outside edge of each nearest point where the diagonals run from the centre of the diamond.

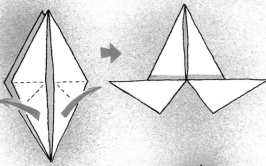

17 Take the nearest of the triangles pointing away from you and fold it lightly towards you and to the right. Turn the 'crane' round and fold the other triangle the same way.

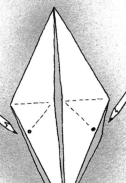

14 Hold down the left side and push a finger between the two layers of the right point at your mark. Lift your mark up and directly away from you and press it flat.

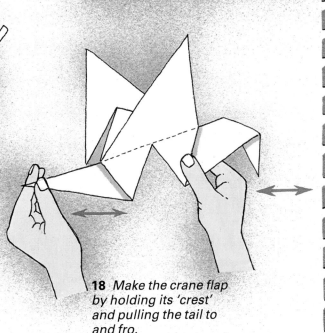

18 Make the crane flap by holding its 'crest' and pulling the tail to and fro.

Paper Architecture

SIMPLE HOUSE

You will need: Heavy paper about 20 cm square • glue or tape • scissors • coloured paper or markers

1 Fold the paper in half from side to side, then in half again the same way. Unfold it.

2 Fold the paper in half from top to bottom, then in half again the same way. It will now be creased into 16 squares. Repeat steps 1 and 2 to loosen folds.

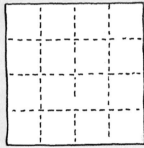

3 With a straight edge towards you, cut along each of the 3 nearest vertical creases to where they meet the first horizontal crease. Repeat on the opposite side.

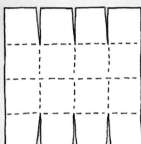

4 Fold the paper between the central flaps on each side so that the flaps cross over each other. Glue them together.

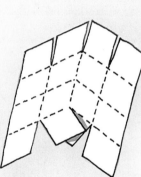

5 To make the walls, fold down the two outer rows of squares so that the end flaps lie across the diagonals of the gable end squares and glue into place. Cut any doors and windows and decorate the walls and roof.

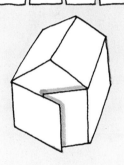

6 To make a chimney, fold a 20 cm by 5 cm piece of paper in half twice to make a 5 cm square. Refold it to make a square tube and glue. Cut a right-angled notch in 2 opposite sides and fix in place.

TOWER AND DRAWBRIDGE

You will need: Heavy paper or light card 20 cm by 40 cm • tape or glue • coloured markers

1 Fold the paper in half then again the same way. Open it out to show 4 10 cm by 20 cm rectangles that will be the walls.

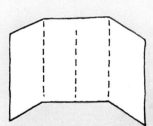

2 Lay the paper flat and draw or cut out any doors or windows. Draw on stonework or cut varying small rectangles of brown or grey paper and stick them in place around windows, doors and over the walls. Draw on ivy as well.

3 Form the tower by folding along the creases into a square tube. Tape securely from the inside.

4 Make 1 cm cuts at 1 cm intervals around the top edge of the tower and fold them inwards as shown.

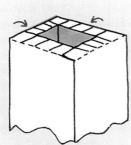

5 Cut a 10 cm square piece of card and glue it to the folded tabs for the roof. Add a trapdoor if desired.

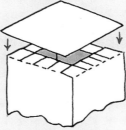

6 Make the battlements from a piece of paper 4 cm by about 42 cm. Make cuts 2 cm deep and 2 cm apart along one long edge.

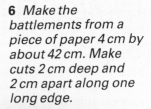

7 Fold over every other flap to form a right angle. Wrap the strip around the top of the tower, creasing the corners, so that it rests on the tabs. Glue or tape in place.

8 To make a drawbridge, cut a piece of card to the height of the doorway and 2 cm wider. Draw on planks.

9 Pierce 2 small holes in the corners of one end. Tape the other end to the base of the doorway. Make 2 holes above the doorway and 2 in the roof on the same side.

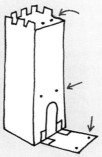
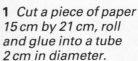
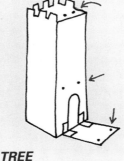
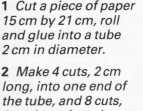

10 Take 60 cm of thread, push it down through one of the drawbridge holes and up through the other. Push each end through the holes above the door then up through the holes in the roof and tie together. Pull to work the drawbridge.

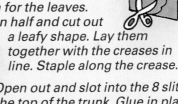

TREE

You will need: Heavy paper • card • scissors • glue • stapler

1 Cut a piece of paper 15 cm by 21 cm, roll and glue into a tube 2 cm in diameter.

2 Make 4 cuts, 2 cm long, into one end of the tube, and 8 cuts, 3 cm long, into the other end.

3 Use 4 sheets of paper about 15 cm by 20 cm for the leaves. Fold in half and cut out a leafy shape. Lay them together with the creases in line. Staple along the crease.

4 Open out and slot into the 8 slits in the top of the trunk. Glue in place.

5 Glue the roots to a piece of card.

IN THE THEATRE

YOUR OWN THEATRE

You will need: Cardboard box • scissors • paper • paints • coloured paper

Cut off the flaps of the box – the open end will be the stage front. Cut 3 long strips 2.5 cm wide at each side to work the puppets through. Then cut 2 slits 1.5 cm wide in the top for scenery. It might be easier if you ask

your parents to cut these with a sharp knife.

Cut another slit across the top near the front for a curtain. Cut a piece of coloured paper as wide as the slit and 3 cm higher than the box. Simply slide this up and down as a curtain.

Use coloured paper or paint to decorate the stage floor, and cut an arch from a large piece of card to decorate the front of the theatre.

Scenery

Measure the inside size of the stage and cut backdrop scenery from lightweight card. Make it 3 cm higher than the box so that you can lift it out easily. The scenery for the nearest slit to the front should be open in the middle to show the backdrop. You can make spare sets of scenery decorated in different ways to suit your plays.

The play

Decide what play you are going to do before you make your puppets and scenery. Invent your own to tell different stories using the same characters and settings.

When you are deciding on a play, think about who is going to work the puppets so you don't get in a muddle trying to operate too many puppets at once. Remember that you can only work one puppet at a time if they have moving legs.

Hints and tips

If you can stand your theatre on the narrow end of a table top it will give you plenty of room to operate the puppets. Use a cassette recorder to provide music or sound effects for added atmosphere.

Lighting

You can create dramatic effects quite easily by using a portable reading lamp to light the front of the stage. This is especially effective if you darken the room, but make sure it is not in the audience's way. You can make coloured lights by fixing coloured cellophane over a torch and shining it down from the scenery slots.

Sound effects

You can add realism to your plays with some simple sound effects. Two upturned empty yoghurt pots can sound like horses' hooves if you knock them on the table. Crumpling cellophane or empty crisp bags sounds like a roaring fire.

If there is a storm in your play, shake a large piece of stiff card and it can sound like thunder, or trickle uncooked rice onto a baking tray for the sound of rain. A tin with a lid filled with small pebbles sounds like marching feet if you jerk it up and down slowly.

A damp cork rubbed slowly down an empty bottle can imitate squeaky floor boards or door hinges. Experiment with different things to see what other kinds of noises you can imitate.

IN THE THEATRE (2)

PUPPETS

You will need: Lightweight card or heavy paper • paper fasteners • paints or markers • scissors

When making your puppets, remember to keep them in scale with the stage and each other. Draw the heads and bodies of the characters on the card and cut them out. Cut out the legs separately and attach them loosely to the bodies with fasteners.

Cut 2 stiff strips of card 1 cm wide and 3 cm longer than the stage width for each puppet. Glue the end of a strip to each foot. With four-legged animals you should fasten back and front legs on each side to each strip.

Colour both sides of the puppet if you want them to enter from either side. Don't draw in too much detail as the audience will not be able to see it. Cloaks and hats can be made so that they can be taken off or changed around.

The puppets are made to walk by moving the 2 strips backwards and forwards as they slide across the stage. Puppets without legs, such as a woman with a long dress, snakes or flying creatures, need only a single strip.

Going Solo

If you want to put on a play by yourself, you will have to make simpler, non-walking puppets that can stand up by themselves. Cut out your figures in one piece leaving a small tab on the bottom of each foot. Then cut a strip for each, 3 cm longer than the stage width and no wider than the slots in the sides of the theatre.

Bend one foot tab forward and the other back and glue them to the flat side of the strip. For an animal, stick 2 legs forward and 2 back. It is a good idea to twitch each character as they speak so that the audience knows who is talking. For crowd scenes, you can draw a group of figures, cut them out and fix them on a single strip.

SHADOW SHOW

You will need: A sheet ● a table ● 2 chairs ● a strong lamp ● thin card ● paper fasteners ● thin sticks and small screw hooks or stiff wire ● fuse wire

The shadow screen
Place the table with a long side towards the audience. Cover the table with an old cloth or blanket and stand the chairs on either end of the table with the backs outwards. Tie the sheet from one back to the other for a screen, making sure it is as tight as possible without pulling the chairs over.

Place the lamp on a large box to shine as directly as possible on your side of the sheet, but far enough back to allow yourself room to operate the puppets. The room must be darkened for the show. You can use music or sound effects to dramatise your show.

The puppets
The puppets are operated by placing them between the lamp and the screen. The audience will see only their shadows moving across the sheet. Remember that the nearer the screen you hold them, the sharper their shadows will be.

Make 2 small holes in the centre of the heads and hands. Cut a piece of wire for each pair of holes and poke one end through each hole. Twist the ends together securely to form a loose loop. Screw a hook into the end of each stick or bend the end of stiff wire into a hook and attach to the small wire loops.

Use the sticks or wire to move your puppets. For variety, use twisting movements as well as up and down ones.

PAPER DECORATIONS

SIX-POINTED SNOWFLAKE

You will need: Thin white paper • scissors

1 Take a square piece of paper and fold it in half corner to corner, creasing it firmly. Open it out and fold the other 2 corners together to make a triangle.

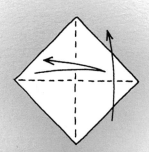

2 With the folded edge towards you fold the right hand point to the left then fold the left hand point over this, to the right.

3 Gently pull these 2 points apart until where they cross is exactly on the centre crease of the paper behind. Then press flat.

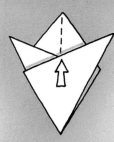

4 Fold the whole shape in half from left to right along the vertical centre crease and crease firmly.

5 Cut off all the points along the edge of the layers which sandwich them. You should now have a wide triangle.

6 Use scissors to cut any shape you like from the triangle. Make sure that you cut through all layers but DO NOT CUT from one fold to the other.

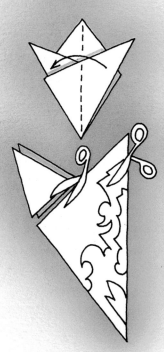

7 Unfold the triangle carefully and you will have a perfect giant snowflake.

FIVE-POINTED STAR

You will need: 8 cm square of paper • scissors

1 Follow steps 1–3 for making a six-pointed snowflake. Unfold the flap pointing to the right.

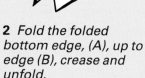

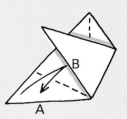

2 Fold the folded bottom edge, (A), up to edge (B), crease and unfold.

3 Slide edge (B) downwards so that it now lies along this new crease, (C), and press flat.

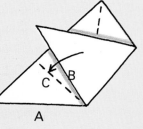

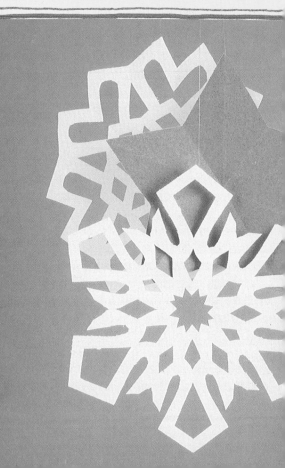

4 Fold the right hand flap so that the bottom edge (B) lies on top of its right hand edge (D).

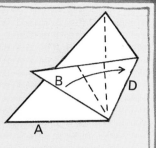

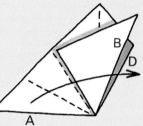

5 Fold edge (A) up and to the right over the previous fold.

6 Fold its point up and back so that the new fold lies on top of edges (B) and (D).

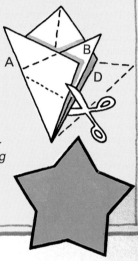

...across the shape as shown. ...sure that all the layers are in ...angle. The steeper the angle ...r cut, the more pointed the ...s of your star will be. For six- ...d stars just follow the folding ...ctions for the snowflake and ...tting instructions for the

STAINED GLASS WINDOW

You will need: Dark coloured lightweight card ● scissors ● greaseproof paper ● glue

1 Fold the card lengthways and cut a curve from the open side to the top corner of the folded edge.

2 Now draw your designs, choosing shapes that fit together neatly. Leave a space at least 1 cm wide between them, and cut out the shapes through both layers of card at the same time.

3 Unfold the card and glue one side.

4 Spread out the greaseproof paper and carefully press the glued surface of the card on to it. Trim the edges neatly.

5 Use the markers to colour the greaseproof paper, using smooth, even strokes. Use strong colours as they will look paler when light shines through.

6 For a more complicated image, do not fold the card before drawing out your design. You can then make each pane different. You can also use pieces of coloured polythene or cellophane, trimming them to fit each separate pane.

7 Hang in front of a window so that the light can shine through.

PAPER DECORATIONS (2)

ANGEL

You will need: Foil or wrapping paper • thin card • pencil • scissors • tape

1 Copy the pattern shown onto a folded piece of card.

2 Fold the paper or foil in half, lay the straight side of the pattern along the fold and draw round it.

3 Cut the paper or foil neatly just inside the pencil marks. Use long, smooth cuts, turning the paper instead of steering the scissors.

4 Bend the skirt into a loose cone and tape the overlap securely.

5 Bend the arms and head forward slightly and the wings back. You can add other details such as a face, carol book or feathers.

ST. VALENTINE'S DAY HEART BASKET

You will need: Two colours of heavy paper (preferably red and white) • scissors

1 Cut a piece 8 cm by 24 cm from each coloured sheet. You can make larger or smaller baskets but keep this proportion of 1 : 3. Fold each piece in half widthways.

2 Place one on top of the other and hold firmly in place with the folded edges together. Cutting through all layers, trim the open ends into semicircles by rounding the corners.

3 Measure 9 cm from the folded edges towards the rounded ones and draw a faint line across. Make one cut in the middle up to the line. Make 2 more cuts either side of the middle and 2 cm in from each edge.

4 Hold the 2 pieces of paper at right angles to each other so 2 corners touch. The loops with corners touching are the ones you will weave first.

5 Open the white loop and put the red loop through it.

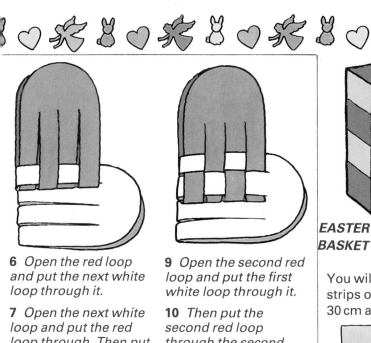

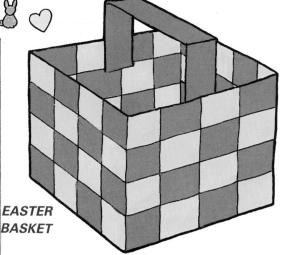

6 Open the red loop and put the next white loop through it.

7 Open the next white loop and put the red loop through. Then put the red loop through the last white one.

8 Slide the red strip up the other piece of paper a little to make room for the next row.

9 Open the second red loop and put the first white loop through it.

10 Then put the second red loop through the second white one. Complete this and the remaining 2 rows the same way.

11 Cut a paper handle 2 cm wide and 15 cm long. Tape each end inside the top of the basket in the middle. Fill it with sweets or flowers for a pretty Valentine's Day present.

EASTER BASKET

You will need: Coloured paper 20 cm square • 4 strips of paper in a contrasting colour 1 cm by 30 cm and 1 strip 1 cm by 20 cm • glue • scissors

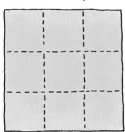

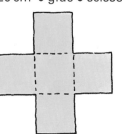

1 Fold the square of paper in thirds one way. Unfold and fold in thirds the other way.

2 Cut out the corners.

3 Fold up the 4 squares to form the sides and cut 3 evenly-spaced slits from top to bottom in each one.

4 Glue the end of one 30 cm strip to the inside of one of the corner verticals. Weave the strip to the next corner. Keeping the verticals upright, crease the corner and glue the strip to the first vertical on the next side of the basket.

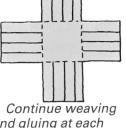

5 Continue weaving and gluing at each corner until you meet the beginning of the strip. Glue end in place.

6 Do the same with the other 3 strips.

7 To make a neat top edge, fold over the verticals that are on the outside of the basket and glue to the inside. Cut off the strips that are on the inside.

8 Use the remaining strip to make a handle then fill the basket with Easter eggs.

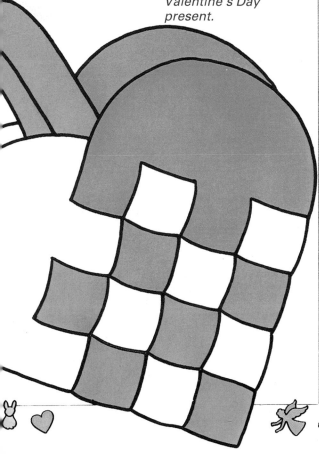

INDEX

Published in 1990 by
Hamlyn Publishing, a division of
The Octopus Publishing Group Limited
Michelin House, 81 Fulham Road, London SW3 6RB

Copyright © 1990 Hamlyn Publishing, a division of
The Octopus Publishing Group Limited

Illustrations: Stuart Brendon

Photographs: David Johnson

ISBN 0 600 56632 3

Printed and bound in Italy